The following pages contain a good deal, but by no means all, of what Jan wrote while she was at Southlands. Her own commentary brings it to life and I will not attempt to add more. But Jan provided much more than written output. She was an inspiring colleague. She led workshops and worship, gave one of the Theological Society lectures, took part in campaigns and kept in touch with the outside world through activities with a variety of churches and other groups. Her stay ended with a "reading" of her work on a summer evening in the College Chapel. The audience from the University, College and beyond was spellbound by a performance that was in turns hilarious, serious and deeply moving. It is impossible to capture such an event adequately in a publication but I believe that what follows goes a long way towards doing so.

Peter Briggs, Principal
December 2006

It was an experiment.

None of us knew what would happen. Southlands had never appointed a Writer in Residence before. I had never been one. We made it up as we went along! And life went on around us: the life of the College and the whole Roehampton University Campus: academic life, student life, street life, wildlife. What should a Writer in Residence do but observe and record all this richness? And maybe also ask 'Why?' and 'What difference will it make?'

I'm very grateful to the College for giving me the original opportunity, through Southlands Methodist Centre, for providing spacious accommodation and – very important – a room of my own to write in; to the Chaplaincy for its hospitality; to staff for their friendship; to the Governors for having the idea and backing it, in spite of the inevitable tendency of creativity to anarchy; to Peter the Principal and Rob the Chaplain, to whom I was accountable for their support without (visibly) turning a hair…

Did my presence and writing on site for nearly five months make a difference to the larger picture? Maybe a small one.

Writer in Residence: a narrative

What does it take?

Take a maker, worker with words,
a migrant writer, with poetic
propensity.

Take a new university, new ideas,
new media, new citizens of the world's
immensity.

Make it spring, with trees in bud and bloom,
birdsong, student politics: all that
intensity.

Make it here, make words appear
on the web, on the walls, on pages scattered
like March petals across a campus of high
duck-density.

Is that all it would take?
What difference will it make?
We'll see.
We'll see.

Soon after I arrived in January, I was taking my daily walk around the campus, enjoying the winter beauty of the big mature trees which were carefully left in place as the buildings had gone up. But I noticed that many of them were disfigured by signs nailed to their trunks – mostly about parking. I wrote this piece and – while trying to invent an ecologically sensitive way to attach it to a tree – gave the Principal, a copy. I believe it was read at an Estates meeting. It may even have been minuted. Who knows the long term effect?

I am a tree

I am a tree.
Not a motorway gantry,
not a bill-board,
not a road-sign,
not a piece of street furniture,
not an obstruction.

I am older than you
and I have been here longer
than these buildings, these roads,
these regulations, this urgency
about parking places; I know
there are more important things.

I breathe life:
your cars, death;
your nails wound me,
your signs degrade me.
I may be a vegetable
but I have my pride.

I am alive:
my roots go deep.
See how my branches
stretch above your head:
respect my dignity.
Accept my blessing.

Walking and watching the world, reflectively, often prayerfully, is a daily part of my life in the Hebrides, developed during my time working at the Abbey in Iona and now in Mull, where I've made my home. Here are a couple of pieces which are not simply 'nature poems', but about human community.

A given day on Mull

After the storm
there came a day
as mild as milk –

the estuary flat calm,
herons rapt
in their reflections.

Where the sun
laid a warm hand,
folk met in the street

and told the story of the wind's fury
through which each had travelled
alone in the dark –
barricaded behind doors
hail spitting on the windows
gusts booming in the chimneys.

Now, meeting face to face,
found being listened to
as sweet as honey.

Overhead, an eggshell sky
cloud-feathered, on still water
a raft of eider duck;

it was a given day,
intimate, precious and enduring:
like a painting on silk.

The Baptist cave, Ardalanish

What did you go out
into the wilderness to see?
A reed shaken by the wind?
Blackface sheep that stop and stare?
Cold waves falling on the long strand?
Brightness ebbing from the air?

Or this grey rugged stone
standing alone, scarred by time,
with lichen like wild hair.
With one fallen, part of a ritual long lost,
incoherent now: *Clachan nan Uamh,*
named not for its meaning, its why,
but its place in the world, its where.

In the cave behind, in an age
of less tolerance or apathy
a dissident preacher took refuge,
dismissed from his job,
turned out of a tied cottage with his family,
bedding down in bracken,
picking a living from the low-tide rocks,
preaching, Sunday by Sunday,
to a congregation of sheep, stones
and like-minded folk.

What did they go out
into the wilderness to see?

A man made articulate by faith and injustice;
hurling words into the teeth of the wind,
with a passion that kept them all warm.

So, even though I had lived in London for 18 years, bringing up a family, returning now, in the 21st century, could well have been a shock to the system.

Returning to London

Returning
after many years
is like falling into a bed
left unmade:

familiar,
frowsty; the air's
heavy with pollution
and insistent noise;

bus lanes now,
travel-cards,
a charge for congestion:
but changing places
is still heavy going.

Returning –
not rewriting
not unravelling
not undoing –

but coming back
to known ground,
a grown woman, and going on
by a different way.

Flight-path

Grumbling overhead –
from right to left
from east to west:
a plane coming in to land
and a plane coming in to land
and a plane coming in to land
and a jumbo jet lumbering overhead,
its engine roar rising and falling
as it descends, minute by minute,
from right to left –
another plane coming in to land.
Packed with passengers:
some glancing down at huddled homes,
most fretting at forced togetherness,
all eager to arrive,
and already looking forward
to finding their own space,
continuing separate journeys –
squads of impatient people
in tired transport:
grumbling overhead,
lumbering overhead,
individuals about to scatter
like seeds from a ripe pod.
    But suddenly,
    those of us on the ground
    glimpse something different –
    flying from left to right –
    a skein of geese
    weft through the warp of a winter sky,
    twelve in formation, purposeful,
    flying together with one mind,
    with powerfully beating wings
    which disturb the air with no-sound.

There were details, though, things observed, which helped to make the connection.

A lot of the poems that began writing themselves seemed to be about birds!

We stand awed under their flight-path –
left to right –
challenged by their counter-culture,
of community on the move:
until they are out of sight
but not out of mind.

Oystercatchers to Oystercards

On the white sand
of Martyr's Bay in Iona
the oystercatchers stand
facing all one way
into a biting north wind,
waiting, patient, grave –
their stance finely calibrated
to each incoming wave
until a sudden surge
or an invisible signal
sets them off with excited cries
flying in a flock
that is both random
and relational.

Under the ad-shell
of a bus stop, beside a busy road
the travellers
facing all one way, in a cold wind
wait for a bus to come –
for the right bus, and in service:
like bingo players hoping
for their number to come up.
And when it arrives at last,
lighted and inviting,
they flock inside, clock their cards
and continue journeys
that are both mundane
and quick with mystery.

Hearing half

The boy on the bus protests

the boy on his mobile on the late-night 72
protests vehemently –

the boy protests too much.

And we can all hear
half the conversation.

Something has happened;
he's explaining.

We all hear his urgent voice
punctuated by silences:

You know it's not like that…
silence

What can I say?
silence

I'd do anything…
silence

We're the best thing that happened to each other…
silence

we are…
silence

we are…
silence

You're breaking up…

silence

And there were bits of human behaviour much less observable on Mull.

So there I was, eavesdropping on conversations, talking to trees. And no-one stopped me. In fact, when people asked 'What does a Writer in Residence do?' I would quote Wordsworth: 'I wandered lonely as a cloud... It can be quite lonely – and, yes, I wander round,' I'd say. 'But, for variety, I can also follow his example at the end of that poem And oft when on my couch I lie, in vacant or in pensive mood. Yes, I can do that, too...'

But of course there was no substitute for being out there, reading the signs – literally, sometimes.

DANGER DEEP WATER

Ice on the pond
(DANGER DEEP WATER)
black oblong
in an expanse of grass
patched with snow.

Two mallards
(was it Valentine's Day they paired?)
having surveyed this
as a nesting place,
finding it stark and unpromising,
sidle into the ornamental shrubs.

Snow crystals scatter from the leaves.

In passing, two students,
hooded against the cold,
snatch a kiss between lectures.

This is just the beginning.

Southlands space

There's a duck on the roof:
a dapper mallard, with damp feet,
looking a little out of place,
looking down into the pond-life
of the quad, for a little space of time:
busy water-boatmen, gnats dancing,
just-awake snails trailing along –
the fertile, murky life of a pond.

Not standing or stagnant water, though,
the four corners are left open,
so that life can flow in and out –
folk of all kinds free to come and go.

Quad, says the duck, *quad:*
but its not a quadrangle
in the Oxbridge sense, with that jangle
of exclusive meanings,

nor is it a cloister, although
it feels a safe space:
sanctuary, but also angularity,
challenge – a paradoxical space.

There's a duck on the roof
watching, then, wings spread, gone
to get on with a duck's otherwise life.

In the college, too, life goes on.

An obsession with ducks began to develop. I learned about the friendly (?) rivalry between Universities throughout Britain, about waterfowl on campus. When I arrived in Roehampton, with its lake, pond, lawns and woodland, it scored highest in the country for duck density. This became the title for a small poetry pamphlet arising from the first half of my time there, a way of saying 'thank-you' to the college. Here's another one from that collection, which draws on insights from Rob Jones, imparted during a pilgrimage we led round the site, about the way the architecture of the new Southlands embodies Arminian theology.

I was being inspired by the place: its architecture, landscapes, inscriptions and sometimes officious notices.

Message to Security: Child Alert

O'er wayward childhood would'st thou hold firm rule
And sun thee in the light of happy faces;
Love hope and patience, these must be thy graces
And in thy own heart let them first keep school.
S.T. Coleridge

Please do not walk
Across the Grass
No games in the
Quad at any time
Thank you
College Notice

The children have landed.
They are playing games in the Quad,
Walking on the Grass,
chasing round the corners,
giggling and falling about
in the shrubbery,
scattering the stones.
One is skipping,
others have brought scooters
as well as violins;
they are playing marbles on the terrace,
hide and seek in the corridors;
they are counting out, who will be on.
And if it's you – what will you do?
    Please do not walk
    Across the Grass
    No Games in the
    Quad at any time
    Thank you
Wayward childhood turns up, takes over the college
every Saturday, to play music. To play.

For them, the firm rule is the discipline of music;
for us, a place coming alive in a different way.

Ah, but, privileged to play – like an allowed fool –
under the discipline of words,
what does a writer do?

I Walked across the Grass
Expecting to be Prosecuted.
I played Word-Games
in the Quad:
No-one noticed – did you?

Subversion is powerless
In the face of Politeness:
Please keep your Creativity
Under Control at all times.

Thank you.

'No one noticed' – and poetry is for sharing. So I started to display what I'd written, first on the door of my office, then finding other appropriate places, like the end of a corridor.

Perspective

At
the
farend
a figure
appears
and begins
to walk this
way, slowly;
the corridor is
very long, with
light filling it from
big windows to the
west and brightness
cascading from above;
outside the clouds unfurl
and under the eaves, wind
whispers, then is overtaken
by sudden impatience of rain;
the sky outside darkens, until
the corridor seems submarine;
voices call from below, feet clatter
on the stairs, bodies jostle from one
seminar room to another; the figure
keeps coming, seeming almost to be
making a statement by slow solitary
walking and now the person who has
all this time been walking down the long
corridor, arrives, avoiding eye contact, and
wordless, thinking
of something else entirely,
turns
through a door
and is
gone
rain runs down the windows
outside, unravelling clouds;
inside, a silent perspective,
spring light filling the space:
the corridor empty, until
at
the
farend
a figure
appears

Monday
The ornamental pool
is filled with milk –
white petals from the cherries.

Tuesday
Down Froebel drive, angry words;
palms-down, the cedars
deny all knowledge.

Wednesday
Thrush calls to thrush across the campus
claiming their space
from tree to tree.

Thursday
On Digby Pond,
ducklings are swimming in circles
Like wind-up bath-toys.

Friday
Overcast evening, a strange duet:
blackbird's flute,
magpie's maracas

Saturday
Look into the heart of Southlands:
a woman and child
are playing.

Then I produced a display of poems printed out with pictures; we borrowed display boards and put it up in the Chaplaincy. Those who feel at home there read my offerings. But I doubt they made much impact on most of the student body, whose visits are brief, between lectures, and focused on meeting friends or buying fair-trade chocolate. I needed to go where the people were. Poetry belongs in the middle of daily life. So I took an initiative with Aishah, the Administrator on Reception. Since everyone in Southlands, staff and students, came to her window to ask for post, would it be possible to post a poem a day on the glass there? I am grateful for her cheerful openness to this suggestion.

A poem a day certainly kept me on my toes. One week it turned out to be haiku.

Towards the end of my time at Southlands, I realised that I was much more likely to have conversations about daily life and things I had written with the support staff than with lecturers, who, preoccupied, passed me, on the stairs. I wanted to celebrate the flesh and blood folk at the heart of the college community.

Each day is its own poem

For the Southlands Support Staff

Jo

O Jo, it was you
who noticed I'd missed a day
in posting up these poems.

An eye for detail
is helpful in someone who cleans,
bringing order to chaos.

But, and this is vital,
you have an eye for what really matters –
the order of the heart.

What a gift, to help
an institution become human!
So that each day is its own poem.

Tom

That smile –
you put your heart into it,
as you do into this place:
caring for folk and foxes
with feeling, with friendship.

You know how to find a ladder –
eventually –
and how to set one up
between earth and heaven
in a space beyond time,
for you're a poet, too.

Celia

You think I don't know how to make a bed –
I just do it differently.
You smile forgivingly –
and (when I'm not looking) straighten it up.
When I'm back home, housekeeping
in my hit-and miss way,
I'll miss your kind face –
and the pillow in the right place.

Abdi Salam

By 10 am, it's as bright
as a new university should be.
It's recovered from the night
before, the morning-after bad taste
of litter: wrappers from take-away meals,
bottles, broken, unwanted things.
Abdi Salam picks them up, bags them,
takes them away, puts them out of sight.
Look again, and see him:
tall, patient, dignified; dealing, day by day,
with the debris of our privileged lives –
a silent man from Somalia
keeping the site, setting us right.

Aishah

'Did you miss my mouth?'
you asked, after you'd been away.
Of course we did.
Not just the plain speaking
and the strong opinions.
Not just the VOLUME
(developed in the classroom?)
that gives a hard time
to those who just want to creep
into the building, feeling unsociable
or nursing a headache.

You may have noticed the mention of foxes in the piece about Tom, above. I realised that a sense of place includes not only its landscapes (indoors and out) and its people – but the wildlife.

But your knowledge of how vital
greetings are, in connecting people;
your cheerful welcome
for friends and strangers;
your determination to see the best
or to name the worst; your wit;
your relish for people's lives, their diversity;
your delight in finding the common ground;
your conviction that if we can't be human together,
there's no point in being here;
all the words that express this, and then
your breaking smile, like sun
coming from behind a cloud –
unmissable, Aishah, your mouth.

A death in spring

The trees are bare still,
buds swollen, almost painful:
spring has been a long time coming.

Past the pond feet hurry to lectures;
election pamphlets blow, Canada geese heckle
a helicopter clattering overhead.

And only a few feet from the traffic flow,
in the undergrowth like lost property,
a dead fox, its back against a sapling;

death took it suddenly –
before it could drag itself away to a den,
to decent obscurity.

Elegant legs, muzzle, tail-tip,
picked out in black, fur – ruffled by the wind –
orange as marmalade.

Unmourned, I thought: but was wrong
When I said 'a dead fox', people told
of encounters, not just road-kill:

a full grown dog-fox, bold as brass,
sunning itself on a wall,
a vixen playing with her cubs;

cries in the night, parallel pathways:
a whole alternative life –
Tom, who feeds them, may know this one.

Wrong to dismiss it as debris of our tidy lives:
the underside surprises; each connection
with creation deepens our humanity.

In the undergrowth, among opening buds,
as the fox goes back to the earth,
we glimpse God, yes, even in a dead fox.

How many people does it take to shift a dead fox? *

Twenty four hours after this poignant piece, I found myself writing, rather testily.

Starts with a visiting American Professor,
perturbed, polite:
Maybe no-one else has noticed?
Surely something should be done?
He just mentions it.

Then a Writer in Residence,
feeling obscurely responsible
repelled – yet moved –
by death's detail, and its resonance.
She writes a poem.

Then several people, hearing
there's a dead fox on campus,

tell their stories of encounters with wildlife,
anthropomorphic, curious, observant:
They reminisce.

Meanwhile Aishah at Reception
listens (she's good at that) and,
setting the narrative alongside the need
for the corpse to be removed,
picks up the phone.

Then there's the man in Security
who says its more than his job's worth:
you can catch diseases this way!
But he knows who to tell.
He puts down the phone.

Then there's the man
who cares for the local fox families,
feeds them steak and kidney pie,
calls them by name: he can't.
He's asked someone else.

A day passes; the Writer realises
the limitations of poetry:
it can move readers, might move mountains,
but can't move carrion a single inch.
Returns to Reception.

Aishah smiles (she's good at that)
sighs and picks up the phone again.
Someone Else has just gone over the road
he's got a lot on just now.
But he'll be back.

Along comes another security man:
'Ho yus, that fox, know about that.
Someone Else'll deal with it.

S'oright – it's on the list.'
Continues his round.

The housekeepers are really concerned:
cleaning up doesn't include corpses –
but they can see it's a problem.
Apparently what's needed
is a big post bag.

The Writer starts worrying again
is it going to be posted?
To whom would you send a dead fox?
The possibilities are endless.
But she does nothing.

Meanwhile Someone Else comes back
from over the road, collects bag, buries
fox,
and wraps up this little local story
in which many people had a part.
And Aishah reassures us: the job's done.
(She's good at that).

**At least twelve*

A wider definition of wildlife would let me include this favourite.

ASBO

Somewhere round the back
a bunch of dodgy fridges
are hanging about near a skip.

If they had hoods, they'd be up.

It's been made clear to them
that they've nothing to contribute
to the college,
to wholesome life in community.

Very likely, in the kitchens,
they were flouting health and safety;
or maybe they've been dumped
for something more state-of the art.

Either way, they're liabilities.

So, with nothing to lose
they hang about on the margins
waiting to make their mark –
ready to release their CFCs.

End of term

The buds can't contain themselves:
young leaves, unwinding in the sunshine,
drop their wrappers on the grass –
they just don't care.

On the pond, geese are putting themselves about,
shouting the odds.

On the climbing-frame,
children chirrup like chaffinches,
territorial,
while those in the sand-pit wear kepis
to defend them against the sun –
a squad of tiny foreign legionaries.

Ducklings have hatched already,
and are swimming in circles
like wind-up toys.

One squirrel, with the sun in his tail,
showing off to another, shadow-boxes,
and does a back-flip.

Meanwhile the students –
in earnest conversation on the lawn –
suddenly start turning cartwheels.

And, with Easter approaching, a last glimpse of the natural world of the Roehampton Campus.

A brief return to Mull, during the Easter break, gave me space to reflect on the experience of being an outsider – even a welcome one – in an established community. There is so much to learn. But it is also possible that a person who does not belong permanently, who is just passing through, may perceive vividly details that others take for granted. 'Writer in Residence' sounds very established. Maybe the term should be 'Sojourner'.

I came back South to a very quiet, tidy campus. As the students returned, the place came alive again.

The shell

It has been lying empty
dry, silent, dead:
shake it and a little sand will run out;
the sea's somewhere deep inside,
the tide of life –
listen, listen,
or is it just imagination?

An empty house:
rooms, corridors, stairwells,
echoing, hollow;
a college without students –
out of term, out of time,
out of tune, only
a long sigh,
long and lonely, the tide gone out;
backwater for a hermit crab –
feelers withdrawn, claws scuttling
round the corner –
a rock-pool, an empty shell.

Now listen
the tide is coming in:
throb of a working day, beat of blood,
the rhythm of life returning;
doors swinging, feet pounding the stairs
students in pairs and phalanxes,
listen –
voices, news, opinions, greetings;
on mobiles, texting, face-to-face,
handing in assignments, handing out insults,
asking questions –
with words, words, words,
coming out of their shell –

and laughter just round the corner.

The University of Babel

You're no more
Pimps and Hoes
than I'm a May Monarch.

What baffles me,
as we pass each other
on the campus, outside

the loud midnight bar,
is how we, all builders
of this new venture,

this tower of learning,
came to be using
such different words

about ourselves, and why
we're here – communicating
such confusion.

Pastoral

Barefoot on the grass
golden boys and girls, garlanded,
dance laughing around a maypole;
the wind plays cat and mouse
with pink and white petals
scattered by the crowd,
who for a moment
see a pattern to it all.

Golden girls, and flowers,
green grass, beribboned poles:
the signs of life and love and lust,
fade and fall and come to dust;
the crowd scatters, the wind blows
litter against the fence, that stands

What will follow are two separate strands of writing. In one I was following the clues in the detail of campus life. In ceremonies like Whitelands May Day, there were powerful paradoxes as well as pastoral charm: The first poem in this sequence was inspired by a poster for a 'Pimps and Hoes' party which happened on campus on the May Day Weekend.

between this safe space
and the outside world.

But for a moment
we glimpse a pattern to it all:
laughter on the wind,
pink petals among the litter;
and in the safe space
at the back of our minds,
the golden boys and girls, dancing
as though there's no tomorrow.

Whitelands May Day

Eminent Victorians consult their watches
(fob watches from pockets
in waistcoats rather warm
for the spring weather –
the sun always shone in those days):
Is that really the time? 2005?
How gratifying
that the tradition is so much alive!

Eminent Victorians smile benignly
and the May-Queens pass
in procession – a time line,
an apostolic succession –
dressed for an Ideal, as though
the sun always shines (even in 2005).
But their smiles are real:
they are elated, edgy, weary;
they feel
the chill May wind,
living (like us) in the here and now,
being flawed human and fully alive.

May Ball

This is something else:
when big tents were pitched
at the far end of the campus
a dunkirk of small boats took to the lake;
all day, the sound of preparation,
as though for a battle with the old
rules of engagement;
as evening fell, the place was invaded
by folk dressed to kill.

All night, the thud of music
like distant artillery;
behind the lines, here in the quad,
little action, only the full moon
strolling across the lawns;
the whole thing anachronistic, odd,
now, when we know that war
and love can take such different forms.

And one more act to the play:
surreal, at 5 am, first light,
victors and camp-followers
who've made it through the night
appear briefly, with cries, laughter,
in ball-gowns and bow-ties,
dancing, running away across the grass:
like a dissolving dream.

Suddenly the soft focus of time past
shivers, gives way
with smart zoom,
takes on the sharp angles of today.

And the contrasts continued when it came to the May Ball.

There was a wider world outside, and sometimes (like the dancers on the eve of Waterloo) we seemed to be wilfully ignoring it.

Just before Election Day (having cast my postal vote), I went to a hustings in the Union, which Rob Jones, among others, had arranged. The candidates courteously gave their time. The student turn-out was very disappointing. I wondered how many would actually turn out to vote. But what could a Writer in Residence do? I imagined someone standing in a polling booth, surrounded by the invisible presences of those without that option.

Election Fever

Are you going to vote?
No
Why not?
Can't be bothered –
its just politics, innit?

People have died!
What?
- for your right to vote
Is that so?
But we all know
about politicians –
can't trust any of them.

Do you know
Who's standing?
Not really.
What do the parties stand for?
Dunno.
What are you studying?
Citizenship.

The Vote

This booth's not big enough
for all of us.
The officials who check
name and number on your card,
and hand out ballot papers with due caution,
direct one person to each booth;
but as you stand here,
picking up the pencil stub,
be aware
of those looking over your shoulder.

There's a working man,
who had no vote and no voice
for centuries:
illiterate, intelligent,
he could at least have made his mark –
but under the law
no chance.

There's a woman,
quite silent,
she suffered for the struggle,
bedraggled with marching
manhandled, mocked –
lost her voice
shouting against injustice.

There's a prisoner of conscience,
behind bars
somewhere in the world today
for believing in democracy,
wanting to take responsibility –
standing up and claiming
the right to be human.

Look over your shoulder now –
you're not alone.
This booth's not big enough
for all of us.
There's only one ballot paper here
and only you have the vote.

I stuck this poem up on the glass at Southlands Reception. But what else could a Writer in Residence do? I printed it out leaflet size, stuck it up around the college among the ads for musical events and flat-shares. That didn't seem enough. On election day I printed more leaflets, to put on the tables in the cafeteria. But by the time I got there, the place was full. I retreated. Then, with a surge of suffragette spirit, I went from table to table, handing out my poem. And, when I got outside again, shaking, I asked, 'Did I just do that?' But then what else is a Writer in Residence to do?

WAKING UP WHITEHALL

This awareness of significant events beyond the campus included, for me, a commitment to take part in events elsewhere in London. In April, Development groups from many places and Christians from many traditions came together for a vigil to Wake up Whitehall. Again, I sensed that this was not setting the University on fire, though it was good to know that a handful of folk from the Chaplaincies were also taking part – including Emily, one of the musicians from Southlands, who led a workshop in St Margaret's Church, Westminster. I found it all very moving, and in the days that followed it became important to me to find ways of sharing this experience around the campus: hence this sequence.

Why we're here

To sit on the chill stone floor
in an ancient church
and listen to voices from the two-thirds world;
to listen to questions
to share anger
to express hope –
that's why we're here.
It makes up for all those righteous pews,
comfy chairs
and politeness.
It's why we're who we are,
in all our cheerful diversity.

To stand shoulder to shoulder,
moved, moving,
on the edge of dancing
to African drumming
which echoes from the vaulted roof
and rocks the walls of the Abbey –
that makes sense
of church-going.
It reminds us
of who we are:
the people of God on the move.

To be encouraged, excited,
incited to take to the streets;
to go out of that grand doorway,
like royalty, the common people,
together and one by one;
to leave in a great wave
like the start of a marathon –
with a message
for the people in power –

this makes sense;
it's why we're here,
doing our best to be
the human race.

Vigil – images

Having carried their little lights
from all corners of the kingdom –
lanterns and torches and church candles
& household candles in jars from under the stairs –
they share matches to light them,
awkwardly: the last time they did this
was a power-cut.
But this is more of a power surge.

*

Where, on most days,
passers-by are asked for change,
tonight all who pass by
are offered a candle
to light
to hold
to make a difference –
to bring about change.

*

As though crocuses
had burst through the concrete
and into bloom, all down Whitehall
the candles are lit.

*

Your hands cradle a flame
in a homely jam-jar:
the night wind cannot shake it.
Although you tremble
with the strangeness
of being here,
your eyes are steady.

A great crowd keeping silence.
Actions speak louder than words.
This is deafening.

Were you there?

(At 11.45 pm, there was one minute's silence)

Were you there for the silence?
Some of us were streets away
but the silence rolled towards us,
with its own power, and impelled
by the outcry and cheering that followed.

The sound, human; the silence, God-with-us.
Can silence be measured? It goes on.
Listen, it is still there, around, within,
wherever we are: whether or not
we are there for the silence –
the silence is there for us.

Stars, angels

(for Emily)

In St Margaret's Church
look up – there are angels
from one end to the other.
But only those towards the east
are gilded.

Over our heads
there are stars, too, moulded into the plaster
where roof-beams intersect, setting worship
among the singing spheres.
But only those over the chancel
are gilded.

You stand up at the east end,
in the big spaces of this building,

facing a great field of folk
shepherded into pews –
a small shy angel – and you get us
all singing.

How can we be sheepish
when you shine with encouragement?
'You can do it …Cool!' – so we all shine,
and the sound we make is heaven-sent,
unites the church,
tickles the angels,
shakes the stars.

We're transcending, with God's grace,
the hierarchy that fallen human-beings
keep putting into place.
You remind us how amazing we are –
that when we sing we're all pure gold:
we're all angels,
we're all stars.

Embankment

It was a long night; the vigil kept on going;
the crowds ebbed and flowed, tired now,
lugging their big banners, cherishing little lights.

When it became too painful to stand still
I walked the wakeful streets: partygoers,
police, rough sleepers, newspaper vans,
lorries with milk and bread, life going on,
but disconnected. I came to the river

and near the sleeping cyclops of the Eye
I stood, watching the tidal Thames
unfurling itself like a dark silken banner,
stitched with symbols and manifestos –

unreadable in the dark hours. Stubbornly
went on with this night-watch, intimidated
by the traffic's random roar; went on waiting,
wondering why I was there, while sane folk slept.

Then heard a tentative voice over my head
in the dark branches, another answering,
and more and more, declaring to the city
a different way of being: call it hope,
community, connectedness? No, I wept
because, right then, I couldn't find the words
for the first inklings of dawn in the sky
and all the trees of London full of birds.

Wake up call

So you all gathered
in one place
at the heart of the city –
the cold heart –
in the place where power is located
at 4 am,
the time when the world is most awake.
So you all gathered
And then?
Then you made a big noise –
what was it like?
Uninhibited?
Threatening?
Hilarious?
Heartening?
What noise did you make?
What difference will it make?

Now I'm listening, to find out.

Go on, I want to hear
a noise that would wake politicians

from their complacency
and our nation out of its apathy
and shake the institutions.
Make that noise!

Only if you join in.

Bananas

At 5am the stewards brought out bananas –
big boxes
of organic fair trade fruit –
offered freely
handed out,
handed round
tossed to the hands of the hungry crowd.

Surprised
and sharing
we found they were just what we needed:
cold and sweet:
as cold as the streets
as sweet as justice.

You will have gathered that I was frustrated by apathy that I met among the students of the 21st Century. But then I remembered that when I went to university and saw graffiti saying Free Mandela, I thought at first this was an advertisement for washing powder! All of us, besides Whitehall, need to be woken up.

There were other frustrations, and I would not be honest if I didn't mention them. Some were about the technology.

Lament of a Maker

O Roehampton
RU, RU the one
place 4 me –
the place where I should B?
    Writer in Residence:
    a dinosaur
    who uses whole words, sentences even,
    a pen and paper, snail-mail,
    and whose attempts
    to gain credibility by texting
    are rubbish…
against whom, it seems,
technology is conspiring:
PC corrupted,
    accounts disabled,
passwords changed
access to the domain denied.
O woe.
    O Roe
        hampton,
    your good people have made me welcome:
    helping me to find a place
    where I may find a voice.
But finding the right words is not enough –
they must be communicated.
    I am ready now; RU –
    to melt the hard heart of your systems,
    put my hands on the keys,
    unlock the account,
and give me access
to a new domain?

Hermit in Residence

A grotto –
rugged, but tasteful;
rocks stacked up
and hollowed out;
mosses and ferns,
maybe some seashells
embedded in its walls,
adding a nacreous lustre.
A vista –
with crags, to which cling
precarious trees;
birds wheeling,
maybe a waterfall;
to etch on the memory
a horrid prospect,
if possible, Gothic.
A hermit –
a social misfit, maybe;
needs to be willing
to don a habit, live alone,
in return for a roof
over his head
(even a rocky one
with stalactites).
A spirituality
of the wilderness?
No, we're not asking for that;
what this hermit does with his time
does not concern us –
just an agreement
to be there
giving our country estate
A certain gravitas –
and a romantic edge:
improving the property,
raising our game.
You'll appreciate
the unique selling point
of a hermit in residence.

The title there is taken from a mediaeval poem called Lament for the Makars, about poets who had died. Well, I felt very much alive, but sometimes – as I waited for my e-mail account, without which it was hard to communicate with people in the same building, to become active – I felt strangely isolated in my little office. Was I a prisoner in an ivory tower? Not quite; but I was reminded of a fashion that grew up in the eighteenth century, for landed gentry to have their grounds 'improved' with a folly, for instance a gothic and half-ruined hermitage. Then they would advertise for a hermit to live in it. Was I one of these?

Of course my responsibility was to find a way of being there which broke down this isolation. That's why walking the campus, putting up poems in surprising places, taking part in events and talking to folk I met felt so important.

But there was one conversation that came to nothing. This Residency was an experiment. It was an attempt to enhance and enlarge the College as a community. It was not an academic appointment. The University had a new Creative Writing course. I went to evening events they had organised. But though I managed to locate one of the tutors, who was based in Southlands, and made an appointment to meet him, I had the impression that I was a 'wild card', not to be dealt with seriously. There was no response to my direct offering of my published work, or the new material I fly-posted around the place, or invitations to events. Maybe part of the problem was my being based in the Chaplaincy: religion being seen as beyond the pale of academic rigour?

In the end, I invited him to a flyting. Flyting was a mediaeval spectator sport – rival poets insulted each other ingeniously in public. It was not a blood sport – usually. Sadly, there was no response to my e-mail or our invitation to the final reading. So what follows is only one half of a conversation.

The flyting

Real poets wear black leather,
real poets are hard –
not hoodies, but fully-paid up
card-carrying bards.

Real poets write their own rules
rejecting mere rum-te-tum,
they're enigmatic, they're macho –
they're not someone's mum.

Real poets do 'constraints',
and are suspicious of rhyme.
Real poets are somewhere more important
most of the time.

Real poets are Published
in obscure magazines
would they write for you if your granny died?
Get real! In your dreams!

Real poets have street-cred
and cool cynical style;
if you said to one 'meet me in the chapel'
real poet would run a mile.

Real poets find a Writer
in Residence rather absurd:
show me a real poet
and we could have words!

Real poets don't seem to live
in the real world where I'm writing.
I'd like to meet a real poet –
hence this flyting!

Crucible

for David Woodman

Elementary, elemental –
crucibles hold molten metal,
can barely contain what flows out
like lava from a volcano;
underneath are fierce beliefs,
and heated words;
the urge for change, earthed
in experience, turned to radical action.
But here, right now, we're in another
element entirely – airy abstraction.

Agreed, there's work already underway:
courses, curriculum,
it's more than just a twinkle in your eye.
And before too long, what's abstract
will become concrete.
It's not just blether.
Who can sneeze at these issues
when passionate conviction,
eagerness to learn
and academic rigour
sit round a table together?

It hangs in the air
like a question: but this is where,
after all the bidding,
in a year's time there may be bricks and mortar
and big windows, to shed some light
on the matter, and a roof
to keep out the rain –
the hard rain of other priorities,
pouring cold water on great schemes.
This is more than hot air;
has got its feet on the ground;
it's getting there.

However, there were other, much more encouraging contacts. I knew I was part of the College community, when people came up and asked 'Do you do commissions?

I did my best, after listening to them talking about why a particular project or person was unique. Crucible, for example, is an existing piece of academic work in the area of Christian Citizenship and human rights – what I was asked to write about was the possibility of a building to house it. Here's a description of a building I'll probably never see, and of making concepts concrete.

In a very different way, I enjoyed listening to a description, by the Bar Manager, of his mother-in-law, who had just died; then writing about this woman I had never met, but who meant so much to her family.

Out of thin air and in the melting-pot,
this is your crucible just now:
concepts and well-taught courses
combined with elemental forces;
substance shaken, something new forged.
Citizenship, social justice, human rights:
abstract words with raw energy filled,
where real people wrestle with a chaotic world.
Out there, they are breaking the ground:
On this campus, you only have to build.

Molly Corrigan

For Noel Sheridan

Molly, Mammy – call her name
among friends – what is it comes to mind?
A woman generous, God-fearing
and, above all, kind.

In Dunlavin, in the Wicklow mountains,
at home, with her children around,
all her life long, a good neighbour,
a wise woman, feet on the ground.

With a welcome on her lips,
a cigarette behind her ear,
taking pleasure in simple things:
contented she was, sincere.

In the whole of the Wicklow mountains
she made the best currant bread:
kneading, baking, sharing it out:
fulfilled, seeing her children fed.

We were watched over – she prayed for us
at home or in distant places,
calling especially on Jude, the saint
(said she) of hopeless cases.

'You have to puck your own goat,' meaning
'I'm not going to interfere.'
But we knew she was ready to listen,
any time: she had a good ear.

Her advice? Simply 'Say your prayers,
you'll be all right.' Then she'd add
'In a corner, remember, God is good
and the Devil's not too bad.'

I could joke with my mother-in-law –
I couldn't wish for a better –
'Molly,' I'd say, 'You're a rip,' and she laughed.
I'll never forget her.

And I will never forget the conversation that became that poem. This is a selection of some of the very different things written during a very creative few months. It may be that those who were surprised by poems somewhere around Southlands in the first few months of 2005, might have chosen different ones. Or none. While I could go on, this is probably enough to give a flavour, of a period in my life which I enjoyed greatly, and where I was stimulated by an environment new to me to write about light hearted and very serious things. Maybe it was also a significant and stimulating episode in the much longer life of Southlands College.

Southlands Chapel
a work in progress

Encircling walls;
this is a place to meet,
day by day, to pray,
where strangers are welcome,
coffee is made, biscuits are fair trade!
Like God's embrace
when wanderers come home:
encircling walls.

I want to end with two pieces. One is a work-in-progress. It was intended as lyrics of a song for the final reading, in June – but has not yet found its tune. If a tune were to be found, then the words would need to be refined. But it is also about a solid building – the chapel that stands at the heart of the Southlands Campus, but also a very open place, a work-in-progress itself, for the Chaplaincy is not the place but the people.

With friends around
this is where to share
laughter and tears
where questions, doubts and fears
are not denied, but faced;
yes, may this be a place
to grow in faith and depth,
with friends around.

Within the world
this is where we must live:
engaged, not set apart;
the yeast must work,
then worship at the heart
starts to make sense
to those who wander by –
and wonder why –
in the round world.

Break down the walls:
this is where we set out
to follow in God's Way.
May this safe place give heart
to walkers in the dark.
May we let go
so, like a seed,
new life will germinate –
break down the walls.